A COMPANION GUIDE TO
Calm My Anxious Heart

My Journey to Contentment

LINDA DILLOW

NAVPRESS

Discipleship Inside Out™

NAVPRESS

Discipleship Inside Out™

NavPress is the publishing ministry of The Navigators, an international Christian organization and leader in personal spiritual development. NavPress is committed to helping people grow spiritually and enjoy lives of meaning and hope through personal and group resources that are biblically rooted, culturally relevant, and highly practical.

For a free catalog go to www.NavPress.com
or call 1.800.366.7788 in the United States or 1.800.839.4769 in Canada.

ISBN-13: 978-1-60006-186-8

Cover design by studiogearbox.com
Cover image by Pierre-Auguste Renoir
Creative Team: Darla Hightower, Arvid Wallen, Kathy Guist

Printed in the United States of America

3 4 5 6 7 8 9 10 / 14 13 12 11

More Linda Dillow
Bestsellers from NavPress

Satisfy My Thirsty Soul

My Worship Journey

Calm My Anxious Heart

A Deeper Kind of Calm

Intimacy Ignited

Find Calm in the Midst of Chaos

Worry seems to be a part of life. As women, we worry about our children, our friends, our careers, our families, our spouses—the list could go on and on. Yes, we want to be content and trust God with our worries, but it's a struggle to let go and free ourselves from the burden of anxiety.

Designed to be used as a companion to *Calm My Anxious Heart*, this journal will help you pause to focus on God's gentle leading in your life. By reflecting on His Word, you'll gain new insights and encouragement, allowing you to let go of anxiety and experience the contentment that comes from trusting God.

Introduction

But this I call to mind, and therefore I have hope: The steadfast love of the LORD never ceases, his mercies never come to
an end; they are new every morning; great is thy faithfulness.
"The LORD is my portion," says my soul, "Therefore I will hope
in Him." (Lamentations 3:21-24, paraphrased by author)

God's mercies are new every morning! His faithfulness is great! Yet
how easy as we walk through our days to forget. *My Journey to Contentment*,
a companion journal for *Calm My Anxious Heart*, will encourage you to call
to mind God's steadfast love, His mercies, His faithfulness, and regain
hope.

Like the Israelites we need memorials to remember what God has
done. When the Israelites crossed the Red Sea on dry ground, God
instructed them to "take up for yourselves twelve stones from here, out
of the middle of the Jordan. . . . Let this be a sign among you . . . a memo-
rial" (Joshua 4:3,6,7, NASB). We easily forget and need "memorials" to
prompt our mind and spirit to remember what God has done for us. *My
Journey to Contentment* is your "twelve stones." As you take time each week
to write down what God is teaching you from His Word and His world,
you will remind yourself of all He has done for you. May He show you
His mercies and love as you discover what it means to be content in all
circumstances.

Each week after you have completed the Bible study for *Calm My
Anxious Heart*, respond to these three items "to remember."

1. What did you learn about God this week?
2. What did you learn about yourself this week?
3. My prayer to "remember" what God has taught me.

Cynthia Heald says that memorizing Scripture increases the Holy Spirit's vocabulary in your life. Although memorization is never easy, you will be grateful you did it when you see the difference it makes in your daily life. Each week there are one or more verses to memorize. If you feel overwhelmed at memorizing more than one verse, just start with one. Then use the Scripture you have memorized to praise God and pray your verses back to God. An example using 1 Peter 5:6-7 follows:

> Humble yourselves, therefore, under the mighty hand of God, that He may exalt you at the proper time, casting all your anxiety upon Him, because He cares for you. (NASB)

My Prayer—Praying 1 Peter 5:6-7 back to God.

> Oh God, I'm not even sure what it means to humble myself under Your sovereign, mighty hand. You ask me to do this so please help me to understand what this means and how I apply it in my everyday life. I am anxious, Lord, and want to cast all my anxieties on You. I can only do this because of Your great love and care for me.

My Praise—Giving praise through 1 Peter 5:6-7.

> God, I give You praise because You are a mighty God. I am humbled as I think of how great You are. Thank You that You say You will lift me up at the time You know is best. I thank You for Your loving care of me. I know You care more about my problem than I do. This amazes me. Because I know this I am able to cast all my concerns on Your strong shoulders. I praise You that You will carry my problems and leave me free from worry.

Storing God's Word in your heart and praying it back to God will keep God's mercies ever before you. Writing down what God is teaching you each week in this journal will help you remember what God has done. Throughout Scripture, we are commanded to "remember." A year from now, when you pull *My Journey to Contentment* off your book shelf, I pray you will be encouraged to remember all God taught you about contentment, and remember that He is the only One who can calm your anxious heart.

—

Ella Spees'
Holy Habit
of
Contentment

Ella Spees' Holy Habit of Contentment:

- Never allow yourself to complain about anything — not even the weather.
- Never picture yourself in any other circumstances or someplace else.
- Never compare your lot with another's.
- Never allow yourself to wish this or that had been otherwise.
- Never dwell on tomorrow—remember that tomorrow is God's, not ours.

MY MEMORY VERSES:

Memorize Philippians 4:11-13 and write it here.

USING MY MEMORY VERSES TO PRAY AND PRAISE GOD

MY PRAYER

Praying Philippians 4:11-13
back to God.

MY PRAISE

Giving Praise to God
through Philippians 4:11-13.

REMEMBERING WHAT GOD HAS TAUGHT ME:

What did I learn about God this week?

THE KING OVER ALL KINGS AND THE MASTER OF ALL MASTERS

God . . . is the blessed controller of all things.

1 TIMOTHY 6:15, PH

LORD, you have assigned me my portion and my cup;
you have made my lot secure.

PSALM 16:5

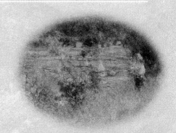

REMEMBERING WHAT GOD HAS TAUGHT ME:

What did I learn about myself this week?

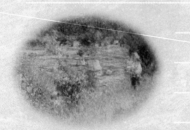

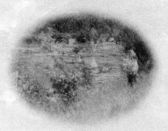

The secret is Christ in me, not me in a different set of circumstances.
—ELISABETH ELLIOT

Remembering What God Has Taught Me:

My prayer to "remember" what God has taught me.

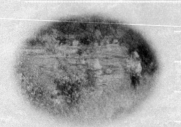

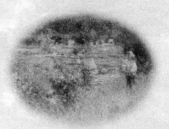

Contentment is a state of the heart, not a state of affairs.
—TIMOTHY SANFORD

Week 2

Content

with

Circumstances

❧

Content with Circumstances

Contentment is a soul sufficiency, a peace separate from our circumstances. Our problem is that our contentment is dependent on our circumstances, on our feelings, on other people. True contentment is separate from our circumstances. It is a choice of the heart. In King Henry VI, Shakespeare poetically describes this internal contentment. A king is wandering in the country and meets two gamekeepers and informs them that he is a king. One of them asks him: "But, if thou be a king, where is thy crown?"

> My crown is in my heart, not on my head;
> Not deck'd with diamonds and Indian stones,
> Nor to be seen; my crown is called content
> A crown it is that seldom kings enjoy.

MY MEMORY VERSES:

Memorize Philippians 4:6-8 and write it here.

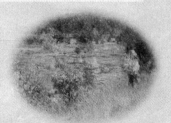

USING MY MEMORY VERSES TO PRAY AND PRAISE GOD

MY PRAYER

Praying Philippians 4:4-8
back to God.

MY PRAISE

Giving Praise to God
through Philippians 4:4-8.

REMEMBERING WHAT GOD HAS TAUGHT ME:

What did I learn about God this week?

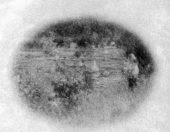

Happiness is something that happens.
Contentment is something we choose.

REMEMBERING WHAT GOD HAS TAUGHT ME:

What did I learn about myself this week?

_____

_____

_____

_____

_____

_____

_____

_____

_____

_____

_____

_____

_____

_____

_____

_____

_____

_____

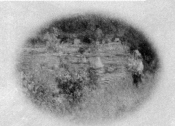

_____

_____

_____

Emerson said, "Beware of what you dwell on for that you shall surely become."

We become what we think. Our thought life—not our circumstances—determines whether we are content. Our thought life—not our husband, our children, our job, our anything—determines our contentment!

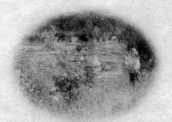

REMEMBERING WHAT GOD HAS TAUGHT ME:

My prayer to "remember" what God has taught me.

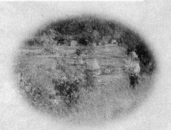

Two women looked through prison bars, one saw mud, the other saw stars.

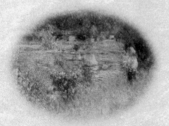

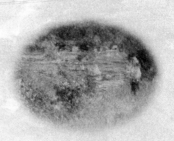

Week 3

———

Content

to Be

Me

Content to Be Me

*For Thou didst form my inward parts; Thou didst weave me in my
mother's womb. I will give thanks to Thee, for I am fearfully and
wonderfully made; wonderful are Thy works, and my soul knows it
very well. My frame was not hidden from Thee, when I was made in
secret. (Psalm 139:13-15, NASB)*

God is painting a picture on the canvas of your life. Your body is
merely the frame. God intends to paint a beautiful picture—a picture of
your character and unique expression of Christ's life to others—and place
it in this frame. But God can't create this work of art without your coop-
eration. It needs to be a joint project between God and you that takes a
lifetime. If you choose to criticize the frame or resist God's brushstokes,
you will not find contentment. It will elude you. If you focus on God's
vision—one that integrates the picture with the frame—and the development of His message through you, you will be "Content to Be Me."

MY MEMORY VERSES:

Memorize Psalm 139:14 and write it here.

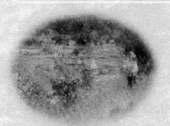

USING MY MEMORY VERSES TO PRAY AND PRAISE GOD

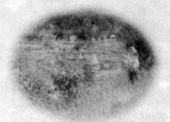

MY PRAYER

Praying Psalm 139:14
back to God.
(Use all of Psalm 139 if you like)

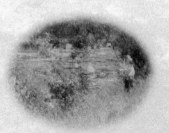

MY PRAISE

Giving Praise to God
through Psalm 139:14.
(Use all of Psalm 139 if you like)

REMEMBERING WHAT GOD HAS TAUGHT ME:

What did I learn about God this week?

Your hands shaped me and made me. . . . Remember that you molded me like clay. . . . Did you not clothe me with skin and flesh and knit me together with bones and sinews?

JOB 10:8-11

REMEMBERING WHAT GOD HAS TAUGHT ME:

What did I learn about myself this week?

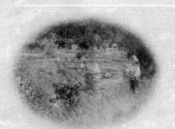

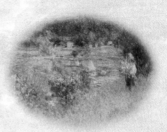

I would rather be what God chose to make me than the most glorious creature that I could think of; for to have been thought about, born in God's thought, and then made by God, is the dearest, grandest, and most precious thing in all thinking.

—GEORGE MACDONALD

REMEMBERING WHAT GOD HAS TAUGHT ME:

My prayer to "remember" what God has taught me.

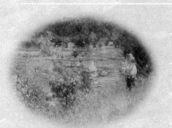

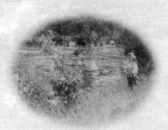

God created our inmost being and fashioned us in our mother's womb so we might be equipped to fulfill the plan that He set out for us even before we were born. Who you are is not a biological accident. What you are is not a circumstantial accident. God planned both for you.

—JERRY BRIDGES

Week 4

———

Content
with
My Role

❧

Content with My Role

Single women look at married women and wish for a husband. Married women look at their husbands and wish for different ones! Is it possible to be content in the role God has assigned you? Childless women long for children and mothers long for the day when their kids will be in school. Is it possible to be content in the here and now?

Elisabeth Elliot has experienced all the roles: single, married, widowed, married a second time and again widowed, and married a third time. She has played all the roles gracefully because she believes each role is a gift of God. Her attitude of trust and acceptance brought a peace beyond comprehension.

What is your portion, your assigned role from God? Have you come to the place of acceptance? To the place of peace and contentment with where God has you? There are positives and negatives in every role, in the life of every woman. Contentment is more a shift in attitude than a change in circumstances. Will you trust God that your assigned cup and portion comes from His loving hands? Will you choose to use your role as a place to serve others?

MY MEMORY VERSES:

*Memorize Matthew 20:28 and 1 Corinthians 4:1
and write them here.*

USING MY MEMORY VERSES TO PRAY AND PRAISE GOD

MY PRAYER

Praying Matthew 20:28 and
1 Corinthians 4:1
back to God.

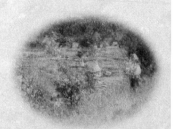

MY PRAISE

Giving Praise to God
through Matthew 20:28 and
1 Corinthians 4:1.

REMEMBERING WHAT GOD
HAS TAUGHT ME:

What did I learn about God this week?

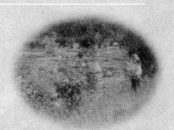

If we're trusting God that His portion for us is best, we can make the secret choices that will bring us a heart of contentment. If we don't accept God's portion for us, we will become women with spirits of discontent.

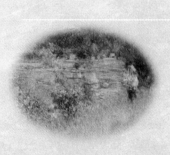

REMEMBERING WHAT GOD HAS TAUGHT ME:

What did I learn about myself this week?

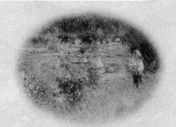

Jesus humbled Himself and took the role of a servant. He used His assigned role to minister to those around Him and to give the ultimate gift of His very life. I don't think many of us have ever thought about this before, and yet if we did, I believe our attitudes would be transformed. We would begin to see our role as a place of service.

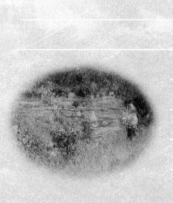

REMEMBERING WHAT GOD HAS TAUGHT ME:

My prayer to "remember" what God has taught me.

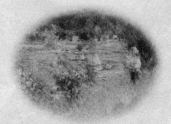

Jesus asks you and me to enter our world to serve others. Is giving your goal or are you waiting to give until God gives you what you want?

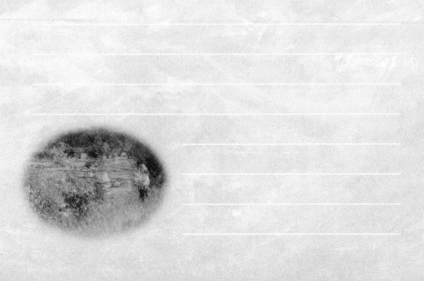

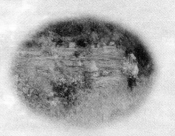

Week 5

———

Content

in

Relationships

Content in Relationships

Let love be without hypocrisy. Abhor what is evil; cling to what is good. Be devoted to one another in brotherly love; give preference to one another in honor.... Bless those who persecute you; bless and curse not. If possible, so far as it depends on you, be at peace with all men.... (Romans 12:9,10,14,18, NASB)

We're commanded in Scripture to love one another, to serve and encourage one another. When these commandments are obeyed, relationships bring joy and beauty to life. Nothing is so wonderful as the love of a husband, a friend. And nothing is as traumatic as the betrayal of that love. One woman said, "I could be content if I just didn't have to relate to people!"

You can't control others: husband, children, friends, roommate, coworker, or relatives. You can't make choices for them, only for yourself. You can trust God. You can control you! You can do your part to pursue peace in relationships and that brings contentment to your heart!

MY MEMORY VERSES:

Memorize Colossians 3:12-14 and write it here.

USING MY MEMORY VERSES TO PRAY AND PRAISE GOD

MY PRAYER

Praying Colossians 3:12-14
back to God.

MY PRAISE

Giving Praise to God
through Colossians 3:12-14.

REMEMBERING WHAT GOD HAS TAUGHT ME:

What did I learn about God this week?

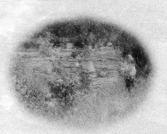

There is no torment like the inner torment of bitterness, which is the byproduct of an unforgiving spirit. It refuses to be soothed, it refuses to be healed, it refuses to forget. There is no prison more damaging than the bars of bitterness which will not let the battle end.

—CHARLES SWINDOLL

REMEMBERING WHAT GOD HAS TAUGHT ME:

What did I learn about myself this week?

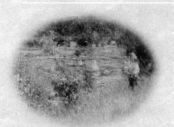

One day Clara Barton, the founder of the American Red Cross, was reminded of a vicious deed that someone had done to her years before. But she acted as if she had never heard of the incident! "Don't you remember it?" her friend asked. "No," came Barton's reply, "I distinctly remember forgetting it."

REMEMBERING WHAT GOD HAS TAUGHT ME:

My prayer to "remember" what God has taught me.

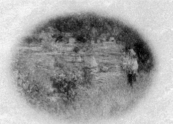

Forgiveness is the key that unlocks the door of resentment and the handcuffs of hate. Forgiveness breaks the chains of bitterness and shackles of selfishness.

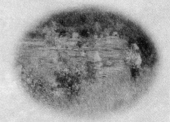

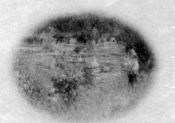

Week 6

Never

Enough

Never Enough

"Do not store up for yourselves treasures on earth, where moth and rust destroy, and where thieves break in and steal. But store up for yourselves treasures in heaven, where moth and rust do not destroy, and where thieves do not break in and steal. For where your treasure is, there your heart will be also." (Matthew 6:19-21)

Billy Graham said, "Our hearts aren't satisfied by materialism. They can't be." When a woman looks for contentment in material possessions, the "things" she wants pull her deeper and deeper into discontent. That for which she longs gradually becomes that to which she belongs. Proverbs describes greed as a leech crying "Give, Give," "More, More," "Now, Now." Not a pretty picture but an apt description. God hates greed. Yet it is rampant. The leech lurks at all our doors.

Not only do we want what others have, our expectations continue to escalate to more, better, and easier. Greed builds a barrier that keeps us from becoming content with what God has given. Sadly, greed is a downward spiral that leads to envy. Envy leads to debt. All lead to discontent.

Where is your treasure? Where is your heart? God has made it plain — we are to be content with what we have. If we continue in a "more, more" mentality, we won't become content. Happiness is getting what we want. Contentment is wanting what we get.

My Memory Verses:

Memorize Hebrews 13:5 and Psalm 119:14 and write them here.

USING MY MEMORY VERSES TO PRAY AND PRAISE GOD

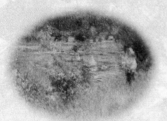

MY PRAYER

Praying Hebrews 13:5 and
Psalm 119:14
back to God.

MY PRAISE

Giving Praise to God
through Hebrews 13:5 and
Psalm 119:14.

REMEMBERING WHAT GOD
HAS TAUGHT ME:

What did I learn about God this week?

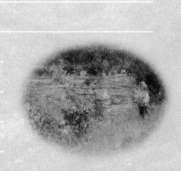

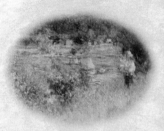

Give a man everything he wants and at that moment everything
will not be everything.

—IMMANUEL KANT

REMEMBERING WHAT GOD HAS TAUGHT ME:

What did I learn about myself this week?

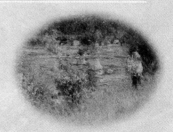

The material wealth we have is on loan to us from God. He owns it all. We do not. Therefore, the question we need to ponder is not, "How much should I give?" but "How much should I keep?"

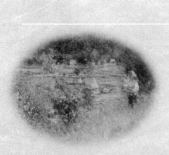

REMEMBERING WHAT GOD HAS TAUGHT ME:

My prayer to "remember" what God has taught me.

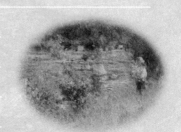

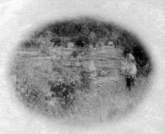

Within the human heart things have taken over. God's gifts now take
the place of God, and the whole course of nature is upset by
the monstrous substitution.

—A. W. TOZER

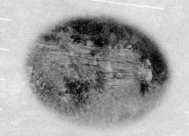

A Faulty

Focus

A Faulty Focus

Imagine for a moment that you are flying to an exotic island. An hour or so into the flight the pilot announces over the intercom: "I have some good news and some bad news. The bad news is our radio is out and our navigational equipment is damaged. The good news is we have a tail wind so wherever we are going, we'll get there at a rate of six hundred miles an hour." While we laugh at the irony, the sad truth is that too often, we fly along like this plane—directionless, but propelled swiftly along by the winds of circumstances.

Our faulty focus must be changed to a fixed focus. We must choose who we want to become and know where we are going. One woman chose as her life purpose statement: "I want to live, *purposely, faithfully, creatively*, and *paradoxically*." Who do you desire to become?

MY MEMORY VERSES:

Memorize Ephesians 5:15-17 from your Bible or from the Phillips translation. Write it here.

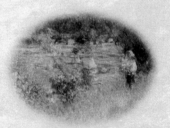

USING MY MEMORY VERSES TO PRAY AND PRAISE GOD

MY PRAYER

Praying Ephesians 5:15-17
back to God.

MY PRAISE

Giving Praise to God
through Ephesians 5:15-17.

REMEMBERING WHAT GOD HAS TAUGHT ME:

What did I learn about God this week?

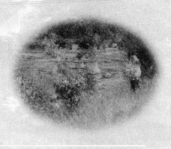

Americans are notoriously shortsighted. We live in a state of myopic mania that blurs the future. The horizon is never visible in the middle of a dust storm. But we must have a vision that extends beyond tomorrow. Living only week to week is like a dot-to-dot life.

—RICHARD SWENSON

REMEMBERING WHAT GOD HAS TAUGHT ME:

What did I learn about myself this week?

_____

_____

_____

_____

_____

_____

_____

_____

_____

_____

_____

_____

_____

_____

_____

_____

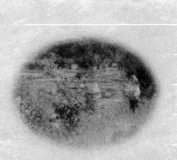

_____

_____

_____

If we haven't chosen what we are living for, we are living our lives by default, acting out the scripts handed to us by family, other people's agendas, and the pressures of circumstances. This is not living as women who know the meaning and purpose of life.

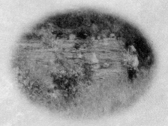

REMEMBERING WHAT GOD HAS TAUGHT ME:

My prayer to "remember" what God has taught me

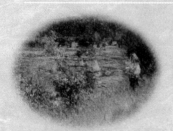

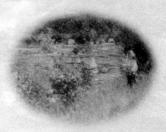

*Things which matter most must never be at the mercy of
things which matter least.*

—GOETHE

Some of us walk as if in a fog when it comes to the kind of woman we
want to become or what our purpose in life is. We spend more time
planning our summer vacation than we do planning our lives.

———

Worry Is Like a Rocking Chair

Worry Is Like a Rocking Chair

Worry is like a rocking chair — it will give you something to do but it won't get you anywhere.

Anxiety is the number one mental illness in America today. One woman said that worry is the advance interest you pay on troubles that seldom come. How true and yet we women are chronic worriers . . . and Christian women among the worst. We say with one breath that we trust God and with the next breath we say how worried we are! We worry because the world is out of control, families are out of control, and we feel out of control. Yet when we are walking in anxiety, we are not walking in faith because worry says, "God can't."

Jesus commanded five times in Matthew 6:25-34 to stop worrying. He clearly said that faith is the answer to anxiety. We must turn our eyes from the problem to the Problem Solver. God desires to calm our anxious hearts!

MY MEMORY VERSES:

Memorize 1 Peter 5:6-7 and write it here.

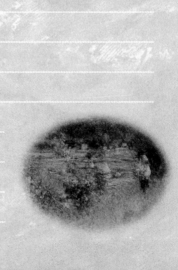

USING MY MEMORY VERSES TO PRAY AND PRAISE GOD

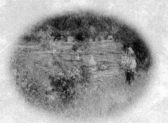

MY PRAYER

Praying 1 Peter 5:6-7
back to God.

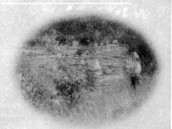

MY PRAISE

Giving Praise to God
through 1 Peter 5:6-7.

REMEMBERING WHAT GOD HAS TAUGHT ME:

What did I learn about God this week?

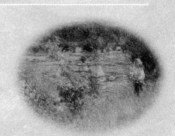

The beginning of anxiety is the end of faith.
The beginning of true faith is the end of anxiety.
—GEORGE MÜLLER

All our fret and worry is caused by calculating without God.
—GEORGE MÜLLER

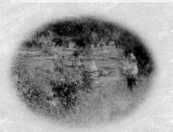

REMEMBERING WHAT GOD HAS TAUGHT ME:

What did I learn about myself this week?

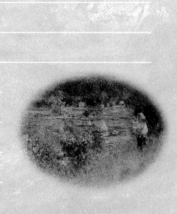

The word *worry* is derived from an old Anglo-Saxon word meaning to strangle or choke. The stranglehold of worry keeps a woman from living a life of contentment and peace.

Anxiety is that which divides and distracts the soul, which diverts us from present duty to weary calculations of how to meet conditions that may never arrive. It is the habit of crossing bridges before we reach them.

REMEMBERING WHAT GOD HAS TAUGHT ME:

My prayer to "remember" what God has taught me.

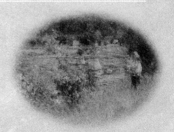

We have moments absolutely free from worry. These brief respites are called panic!

It is not only wrong to worry, it is infidelity, because worrying means that we do not think that God can look after the details of our lives, and it is never anything else that worries us.

—Oswald Chambers

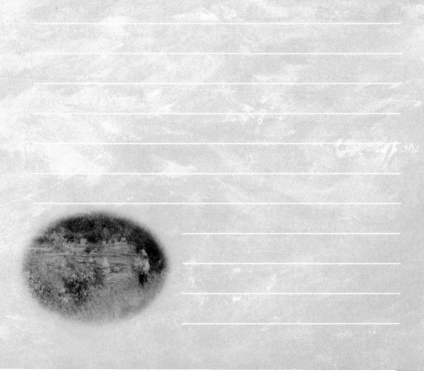

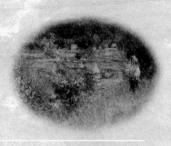

Week 9

—

Faith:
The
Foundation

Faith: The Foundation

Faith is the answer to anxiety. God does not ask that we have blind faith, but abandoned faith, a faith that trusts Him fully. Our faith is based on God's Word, not our feelings. It is rooted in God's marvelous character. Amy Carmichael, missionary to India's children, said her ability to trust God began with her confidence in God's character. She believed that:

- ❧ God is, first and always, a loving Father.
- ❧ God is in control, and everything He allowed into her life was ultimately for her good.
- ❧ As she "tucked" herself into God by trusting Him as a little child, He was able to carry her through all things.

Confidence in God's character enables us to throw ourselves with complete abandon into His care. When we believe He truly is the King of kings, Lord of lords, and Blessed Controller of all things and "tuck" ourselves into Him, our anxious hearts will be calmed.

MY MEMORY VERSES:

Memorize Hebrews 11:1 and write it here.

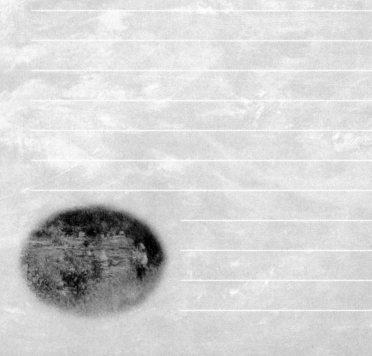

Using My Memory Verses to Pray and Praise God:

My Prayer
Praying Hebrews 11:1 back to God.

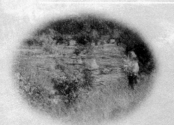

My Praise
Giving Praise to God through Hebrews 11:1.

REMEMBERING WHAT GOD HAS TAUGHT ME:

What did I learn about God this week?

Faith is believing God is true to His Word when my feelings are screaming out something different.

Faith is certain belief in what I know to be true but cannot, at that moment, feel or touch.

Faith is completing my small part of the picture/puzzle without being able to see the finished product.

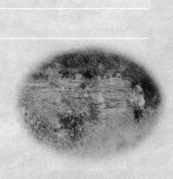

REMEMBERING WHAT GOD
HAS TAUGHT ME:

What did I learn about myself this week?

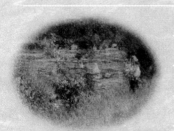

The Problem: Living by Feelings

THE RESULT of living by feelings? An anxious heart!

The Solution: Living by Faith

THE RESULT of living by faith? A calm heart.

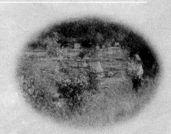

REMEMBERING WHAT GOD HAS TAUGHT ME:

My prayer to "remember" what God has taught me.

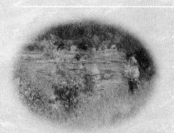

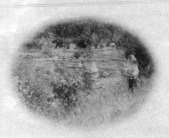

My feelings are strong BUT:
God's Word is truer than anything I feel.
God's Word is truer than anything I experience.
God's Word is truer than any circumstance I will ever face.
—NEY BAILEY

Week 10

Trusting God
with the
What Ifs

Trusting God with the What Ifs

🕏 *What if* I get cancer?

🕏 *What if* my child rebels?

🕏 *What if* we can't pay the mortgage?

🕏 *What if, what if*?

Waiting for the *What Ifs* of life, for what *might* happen, causes the sturdiest of hearts to be anxious. Contentment comes from a proper relationship with God, not a response to the circumstances. Our *What Ifs* will either drive us to God and faith, or drive us to worry and dependence on self. We worry or we trust. God gives peace and contentment, worry gives illness and misery.

Psalm 141:8 encourages us to fix our eyes on our Sovereign Lord and take refuge in Him. Psalm 112:7-8 (NASB) says, "He will not fear evil tidings; His heart is [fixed] steadfast. . . . His heart is upheld, he will not fear." Only as our heart is fixed on our sovereign, loving Lord can we be at peace in the midst of *What Ifs*. How wonderful it is to be assured that as we choose to fix our hearts on God, He, at the same time, upholds our hearts!

MY MEMORY VERSES:

Memorize Jeremiah 17:7-8 and write it here.

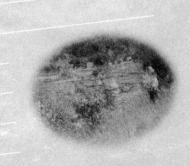

USING MY MEMORY VERSES TO PRAY AND PRAISE GOD

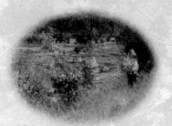

MY PRAYER

Praying Jeremiah 17:7-8
back to God.

MY PRAISE

Giving Praise to God
through Jeremiah 17:7-8.

REMEMBERING WHAT GOD HAS TAUGHT ME:

What did I learn about God this week?

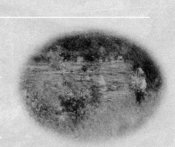

When we turn to control, strategies, intelligence, and manipulation, we are trusting in ourselves. Instead of giving our anxious hearts to God, we handle the uncertainty of the *What Ifs* of life by employing these control tactics to "help God out."

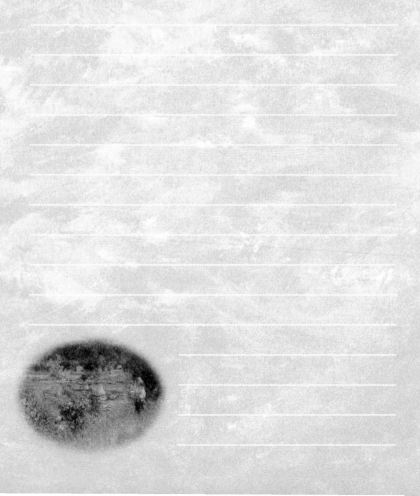

Remembering What God Has Taught Me:

What did I learn about myself this week?

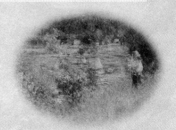

What If is a spiritual disease. It looks to the future and worries about what God might allow. It leads to anxiety.

> *My life has been full of terrible misfortunes, most of which*
> *never happened.*
> —MICHEL MONTAIGNE

REMEMBERING WHAT GOD HAS TAUGHT ME:

My prayer to "remember" what God has taught me.

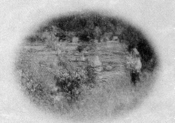

God grant me the serenity to accept that which I cannot change, courage to change the things I can and wisdom to know the difference, living one day at a time, enjoying one moment at a time, accepting hardship as a pathway to peace, taking, as Jesus did, this sinful world as it is, not as I would have it, trusting that You will make all things right if I surrender to Your will, so that I may be reasonably happy in this life and supremely happy with You forever in the next.

—REINHOLD NIEBUHR

Trusting God with the *If Onlys*

Trusting God with the
If Onlys

- *If Only* I had more money
- *If Only* I had gotten that job (house, outfit, award)
- *If Only* my husband were more sensitive

We cripple ourselves spiritually by going over and over the *If Onlys*. The Israelites had the *If Only* griping spirit. They had a problem. (Usually the *If Only* disease comes as a result of a problem.) No water. Instead of focusing on God when the problem came, the people focused on what they didn't have. This led to irrational thinking; they lost all perspective and began to look back on Egypt with longing! When they dwelled on what they didn't have, the one problem mushroomed until they'd compiled a long list of grievances.

We do the same thing. When we fix our eyes on the problem, our minds take one negative and balloon it into many negatives until we have enough balloons to throw a pity party. In order to conquer the *If Only* disease, we must fix our eyes not on the problem but on our great God.

MY MEMORY VERSES:

Memorize Psalm 77:11-14 and write it here.

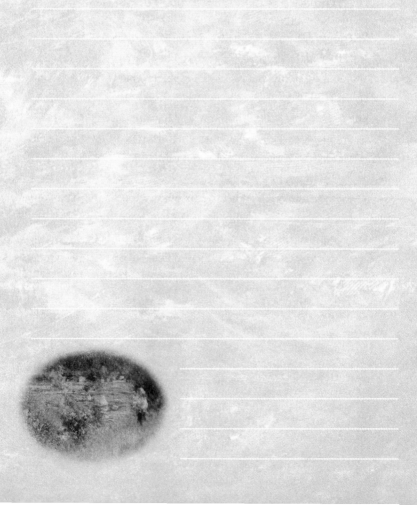

USING MY MEMORY VERSES TO PRAY AND PRAISE GOD

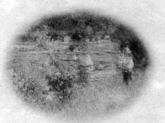

MY PRAYER

Praying Psalm 77:11-14
back to God.

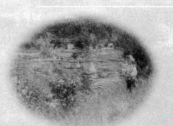

MY PRAISE

Giving Praise to God
through Psalm 77:11-14.

Remembering What God Has Taught Me:

What did I learn about God this week?

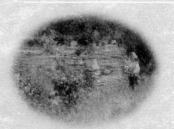

If Only is a spiritual disease. It looks to the past and grumbles about what God has given. It leads to anger.

Contentment floats elusively beyond our grasp in the world of *If Onlys*. *If Only* we had our *If Onlys*, we'd be content!

REMEMBERING WHAT GOD
HAS TAUGHT ME:

What did I learn about myself this week?

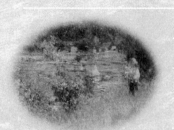

We catch the *If Only* disease when we dwell on what we don't have instead of on what we do have.

REMEMBERING WHAT GOD HAS TAUGHT ME:

My prayer to "remember" what God has taught me.

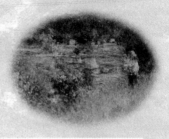

Life can be painful. Most people do not choose this pain; it comes with living. Contentment, however, is different. Contentment or discontent is a matter of the will, a choice. When we choose obedience, God, in His wonderful way with surprises, can redeem the pain and suffering in our lives and can turn the destruction into benefit.

—RICHARD SWENSON

Trusting God
with the
Whys

Trusting God with the *Whys*

*Why dost Thou stand afar off, O LORD? Why dost Thou
hide Thyself in times of trouble?*

(PSALM 10:1, NASB)

Three of the Psalms begin with the question, *Why?* David wasn't the only one to ask *Why?* The Lord Jesus screamed from the cross, *"My God, My God, Why hast Thou forsaken me?"* (Matthew 27:46, NASB). There are multitudes of whys in each of our lives, unanswered questions that tear our hearts in two. Like our Lord Jesus, we must turn our *Whys* into trust.

The bridge that takes us over the many *Whys* is trusting God to be the Blessed Controller of all things (1 Timothy 6:15, PH). He is the Blessed Controller of our circumstances, gifts, abilities, possessions, roles, relationships and all our *Whys*. We acknowledge His sovereign control by trusting Him for everything—what we don't understand, can't see, and what doesn't make sense to us. We accept what He has allowed today. And give all our tomorrows to Him. The inexpressible joy on the other side of yielding all control to Him is contentment and a calm heart.

MY MEMORY VERSES:

Memorize Habakkuk 3:17-19 and write it here.

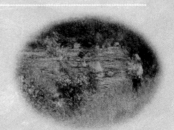

USING MY MEMORY VERSES TO PRAY AND PRAISE GOD

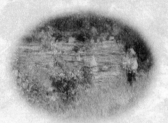

MY PRAYER

Praying Habakkuk 3:17-19
back to God.

MY PRAISE

Giving Praise to God
through Habakkuk 3:17-19.

REMEMBERING WHAT GOD HAS TAUGHT ME:

What did I learn about God this week?

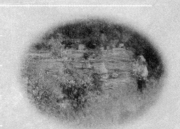

When we humbly yield to God's plan and purpose for our lives, we worship.

The Lord is my peace. I shall not live in anxiety. He puts me under His wing of comfort and calms my spirit within me. He takes all my anxieties on Himself and helps me to focus on Him. Yes, though I walk through a time of grave uncertainties and fierce anxieties, I will not fret—for You are my peace. Your Word and Your presence calm me now. You hold my uncertainties in the palm of Your hand. You soothe my anxious mind— You smooth my wrinkled brow. Surely serenity and trust in You shall fill me all the days of my life. And I shall keep my mind stayed on You forever.

—A PARAPHRASE OF PSALM 23 BY JUDY BOOTH

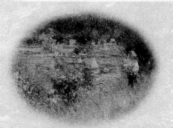

REMEMBERING WHAT GOD
HAS TAUGHT ME:

What did I learn about myself this week?

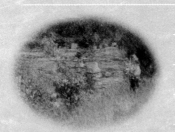

This is the blessed life—not anxious to see far in front, nor eager to choose the path, but quietly following behind the Shepherd, one step at a time. The Shepherd was always out in front of the sheep. He was down in front. Any attack upon them had to take Him into account. Now God is down in front. He is in the tomorrows. It is tomorrow that fills men with dread, God is there already. All the tomorrows of our life have to pass Him before they can get to us.

—F. B. Meyer

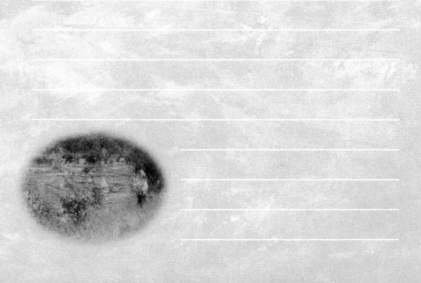

REMEMBERING WHAT GOD HAS TAUGHT ME:

My prayer to "remember" what God has taught me.

Contentment can become an act of worship. Jeremiah Burroughs wrote in 1648 that we worship God more by contentment than when we come to hear a sermon, or spend a half hour in prayer.

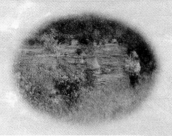

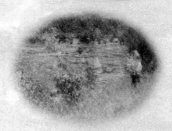

Author

LINDA DILLOW and her husband, Jody, have lived in Europe and Asia and have been involved in international ministry for twenty-five years. Linda speaks at women's retreats and conferences in America, Asia, and Europe.

Her books include *A Deeper Kind of Calm*, *Satisfy My Thirsty Soul*, *Intimate Issues*, and *Intimacy Ignited*, coauthored with Lorraine Pintus. She and her husband now live in Monument, Colorado. They have four grown children and are grandparents.